GW00367597

THEY THINK IT'S ALL OVER

FRANK WORRALL

THEY THINK IT'S ALL OVER

Funny football quotes for the whole family

jb

First published in the UK by John Blake Publishing
an imprint of Bonnier Books UK
4th Floor, Victoria House,
Bloomsbury Square,
London WC1B 4DA

Owned by Bonnier Books
Sveavägen 56, Stockholm, Sweden

www.facebook.com/johnblakebooks
twitter.com/jblakebooks

First published in hardback in 2022

ISBN: 978 1 78946 638 6
eBook: 978 1 78946 672 0

British Library Cataloguing-in-Publication Data:

A catalogue record for this book is available from the British Library.

Design by www.envydesign.co.uk

Printed and bound in Great Britain by Clays Ltd, Elcograf S.p.A.

1 3 5 7 9 10 8 6 4 2

FSC
MIX
Paper from
responsible sources
FSC® C018072
www.fsc.org

John Blake Publishing is an imprint of Bonnier Books UK
www.bonnierbooks.co.uk

This book is dedicated to my great friend,
Dave Morgan

CONTENTS

INTRODUCTION

**It's the gift that keeps on giving – the unerring
ability of football's entertainers, mavericks and
just plain daft buggers to magic up quotes that
leave us in fits of laughter.**

The modern-day game is often dismissed as
having lost its heart: that it is in thrall to greed. That
it has become a money-making machine for many
on and off the pitch who don't deserve the cash
and adulation they demand. That it is no longer the
domain of the working man, but the plaything of a
multibillion-pound industry operating at the behest
of outrageously generous TV deals.

But ask any fans in the legendary citadels of the north and south, such as the Theatre of Dreams (Old Trafford), or the Emirates (Arsenal) or the new White Hart Lane (Spurs), and you'll find a passion that burns brightly.

A true, undying love of the game and its idio-syncrasies.

And those very same fans love it ('just love it!', copyright Kevin Keegan) when someone within the game – be it a footballer, manager or pundit – makes a verbal gaffe. Yes, the competition to be the king (or queen) of football's comedy club is stiff.

Of course, some of its top-level competitors deliberately set out to make a name for themselves. The likes of top contenders such as Neil Warnock, Ian Holloway and Roy Keane are like moths to the proverbial flame when it comes to gags or jibes whenever a mic is pushed in front of them.

These performers have proved themselves so amusing and entertaining that fans I know some-times tune in to watch a match on Sky, the BBC or ITV purely to witness their acts in the studio before a match, after and at half-time. The game itself, remarkably, becomes but a sideshow.

Then we have those masters of off-the-cuff comment who know exactly what outrage or effect their comments will have in print or on the radio. Good interviewees will always sell newspapers and boost audience listening, or viewing, figures and ratings. Like the game itself, they are worth their weight in gold.

Researching this fun book for all the family, I was struck by just how daft certain 'stars' of football can appear in the context of standalone quotes. David Beckham, for instance, has millions in the bank, a brand that continues to attract investors and even his own football club franchise in the States. He is clearly a smart guy. Yet some of his comments would have you believing he's a plank, taking the mickey, or both.

Becks is just one of those apparent buffoons bringing joy in these pages. Other footballers – home and abroad – managers, pundits and refs also take a well-deserved bow. So, grab a cuppa, sit back – and enjoy a giggle at their expense. The extremely well-remunerated players and managers featured in this book can certainly afford it!

FRANK WORRALL
London, 2022

MORE ÉMILE THAN GIANFRANCO (ZOLA)

FOOTBALL'S GREAT THINKERS

'It's not always plain sailing – especially when you're flying.'

BRENDAN RODGERS

'There's no in-between – you're either good or bad. We were in-between.'

GARY LINEKER

'Money isn't the most important thing. It is important, of course. I am not Mahatma Gandhi.'

JÜRGEN KLOPP

'You can't bite yer nose off to spite yer face.'

PAUL MERSON

'We don't have any problems, apart from the problems we have.'

RAFA BENITEZ

'You can't win anything with kids.'

ALAN HANSEN

'If you can't pass the ball properly, a bowl
of pasta is not gonna make that much
difference.'

HARRY REDKNAPP

'People say 'go with the flow', but do you
know what goes with the flow? Dead fish.'

ROY KEANE

'I'm only a human being.'

WAYNE ROONEY

'Football is a simple game – 22 men chase
a ball for 90 minutes and, at the end, the
Germans win.'

GARY LINEKER

'Chairman Mao has never seen a greater show of red strength.'

BILL SHANKLY

'The title race is between two horses and a little horse that needs milk and needs to learn how to jump.'

JOSÉ MOURINHO

'When I arrive at the gates of Heaven, the Lord will ask, 'What did you do in your life?' I will respond, 'I tried to win football matches.' He will say, 'Are you certain that's all?' But, well, that's the story of my life.'

ARSÈNE WENGER

'That was in the past. We're in the future now.'

DAVID BECKHAM

'Rome wasn't built in a day, but I wasn't
on that particular job.'

BRIAN CLOUGH

'Every dog has its day and today is woof
day! Today I just want to bark.'

IAN HOLLOWAY

'Fear is not a word in my football
documentary. Unhappy is a nice word.'

JOSÉ MOURINHO

'Football, hey? Bloody hell.'

**ALEX FERGUSON AFTER MAN UNITED'S LATE
CHAMPIONS LEAGUE FINAL
WIN IN 1999**

'When the seagulls follow the trawler, it is because they think sardines will be thrown into the sea.'

ERIC CANTONA

'Running is for animals. You need a brain and a ball for football.'

LOUIS VAN GAAL

'Sometimes you see beautiful people with no brains. Sometimes you have ugly people who are intelligent, like scientists.'

JOSÉ MOURINHO

'A football team is like a beautiful woman. When you do not tell her, she forgets she is beautiful.'

ARSÈNE WENGER

'Is the Pope Catholic? No, I'm serious.
I really need to know.'

DAVID BECKHAM

'Some people think football is a matter of
life and death. I assure you, it's much more
serious than that.'

BILL SHANKLY

'Aggression is what I do. I go to war.
You don't contest football matches in a
reasonable state of mind.'

ROY KEANE

'For me, pressure is bird flu. I'm serious.
It's not fun and I'm more scared of it than
football. Football is nothing compared with
life. For me, bird flu is the drama of the last
few days. I'll have to buy a mask.'

JOSÉ MOURINHO

'I feel like I've been on *EastEnders* all my life and now I'm playing King Lear.'

IAN HOLLOWAY

'My greatest challenge is not what's happening at the moment. My greatest challenge was knocking Liverpool right off their f*****g perch. And you can print that.'

ALEX FERGUSON

'I am not dealing with footballers, I am dealing with people. They have fears and worry about failing and making fools of themselves in front of 80,000 people. I have to make them see that without each other they are nothing.'

PEP GUARDIOLA

'If God had wanted us to play football in the sky, he'd have put grass up there.'

BRIAN CLOUGH

'I have to walk. If I couldn't, I'd be in a padded cell by now.'

ROY KEANE

'I definitely want Brooklyn to be christened, but I don't know into what religion yet.'

DAVID BECKHAM

'Life only makes sense when our highest ideal is to serve Christ!'

NEYMAR

'I like musicals and I love music.'

WAYNE ROONEY

'I once cried because I had no shoes to play football, but one day I met a man who had no feet.'

ZINEDINE ZIDANE

'In Spain, people have lunch and dinner a lot later. When I return to England, I'll have to eat alone at midnight.'

DAVID BECKHAM

'If you think you're perfect already, then you never will be.'

CRISTIANO RONALDO

'I think I've lost a lot of my gay fans to Gavin Henson. It's a shame because I really love them.'

DAVID BECKHAM

'I used the Olympics in my team talk. When I went to bed, Kelly Holmes turned me on... which is sad for me, isn't it? But when I watched Kelly and the relay lads, their ambition was to aim for the top. Now I think I have a group of lads who should look at themselves and also aim for the top.'

NEIL WARNOCK

'I always wanted to be a footballer. Of course I did. Not a basketball player, as I get asked on a daily basis, or a roofer who doesn't need to use a ladder, or a zookeeper who can talk to the giraffes face to face.'

PETER CROUCH

'Sometimes when you aim for the stars, you hit the moon.'

IAN HOLLOWAY

THE GOOD, THE BAD & THE BUBBLY

PERFORMANCE, SUCCESS AND FAILURE

'After Chelsea scored, Bolton epitulated.'

PAUL MERSON

'Andy Johnson was literally banjoed
out of the game.'

ROY HODGSON

'There's no if, buts or maybes, but Robbie
Keane should have scored.'

ANDY GRAY

'Liverpool have played with no real
convention.'

RAY HOUGHTON

'The ball is like a woman, she loves to be
caressed.'

ERIC CANTONA

'Tottenham have impressed me. They haven't thrown in the towel even though they have been under the gun.'

BOBBY CHARLTON

'I don't need the best hairstyle or the best body. Just give me a ball at my feet and I'll show you what I can do.'

LIONEL MESSI

'There was a spell in the second half when I took my heart off my sleeve and put it in my mouth.'

IAN HOLLOWAY

'Sunderland edged the game by a long, long way for me.'

KEVIN KEEGAN

'First I went left, he did too. Then I went right, and he did too. Then I went left again, and he went to buy a hot dog.'

ZLATAN IBRAHIMOVIĆ ON HIMSELF

'I am searching for abstract ways of expressing reality, abstract forms that will enlighten my own mystery.'

ERIC CANTONA, INTERVIEW WITH THE GUARDIAN, 2003

'My heart was in my hands.'

RICKY SBRAGIA

'Walsall have given City more than one anxious moment amongst many anxious moments.'

DENIS LAW

'From the first day, you are told if you want to be the best then stay out of the nightclubs!'

LIONEL MESSI, ON FACEBOOK

'Preston have an overpass in the middle of the pitch.'

STEVE COTTERILL

'My ceiling's broken, my car's got a puncture and we've just lost two matches. But I've got my health and I'll ask the big man upstairs why he didn't give us a point.'

IAN HOLLOWAY

'Early on in my career I had a lot of bad press about my temperament, but I was only a young lad then.'

WAYNE ROONEY

'We played on a hot day and I was
sweating profoundly.'

MICKY QUINN

'He (Zidane) looks like when he plays, he is
on his sofa, he's so relaxed.'

PATRICE EVRA

'As we say in Portugal, they brought the bus
and they left the bus in front of the goal.'

JOSÉ MOURINHO

'They wear their hearts on their shirts.'

STEVE BULL

'It was a once-in-a-lifetime experience and hopefully I can repeat it on Saturday.'

MIDFIELDER ALFIE POTTER WHEN ON LOAN AT KETTERING

'I don't give a s***e, to be honest. I love to see Chelsea players moaning at the referee, trying to intimidate the officials and José (Mourinho) jumping up and down. It's great to see.'

SAM ALLARDYCE

'Throughout my career I have been pretty successful. I've played for some pretty big teams, represented my country quite a few times – and played for managers without sentiment.'

DAVID BECKHAM

'Manchester City are defending like beavers.'

CHRIS KAMARA

'Louis van Gaal has nothing more to learn.'

LOUS VAN GAAL

'I couldn't be more chuffed if I were a badger at the start of the mating season.'

IAN HOLLWAY

'Look, I'm a coach, I'm not Harry Potter. He is magical, but in reality there is no magic. Magic is fiction and football is real.'

JOSÉ MOURINHO

'Woodcock would have scored, but his shot was too perfect.'

RON ATKINSON

'If you lose a game, everyone asks why this player didn't play. If we win, nobody asks.'

JÜRGEN KLOPP

'When I was at Valencia my wife said we'd win the league. She was right and to celebrate asked me for a new watch. I bought her the watch, but then she said we would win the UEFA Cup and wanted another watch when we won. Now she says we'll win the Champions League – and she will want an even more expensive watch. My wife has a lot of confidence and a

lot of watches.'

RAFA BENITEZ

'To put it in gentleman's terms... if you've been out for a night and you're looking for a young lady and you pull one, some weeks they're good-looking and some weeks they're not the best. Our performance today would have been not the best-looking bird but at least we got her in the taxi...it was still very pleasant and very nice, so thanks very much and let's have coffee.'

IAN HOLLOWAY

'If you don't score and you have chances, you are disappointed.'

WAYNE ROONEY

'In my teams, when we win, we all win, and when we lose, I lose.'

JOSÉ MOURINHO

'We have one or two young players who have done very little in the game. They need to remember that and not slack off. They need to remember just how lucky we all are to play for Manchester United and show that out on the pitch.'

ROY KEANE

'As long as I'm not taking a penalty we will be okay. But if it's like two years ago I will need a doctor.'

RAFA BENITEZ

'We couldn't cope with long-ball United – it was thump it forward and see what they could get.'

SAM ALLARDYCE ON LOUIS VAN GAAL'S MAN UNITED

IT FIGURES ?
(NOT AS A RULE)

SUMMING UP AND ANALYSES

'Derby could have gone into liquidisation.'

MARTIN KEOWN

'Spurs need three or four players – and three or four won't be enough.'

ALAN SHEARER

'I would not be bothered if we lost every game as long as we won the league.'

MARK VIDUKA

'We must have had 99 per cent of the game. It was the other 3 per cent that cost us the match.'

RUUD GULLIT

'If we do not concede, we will go away from the game with at least a point.'

JONNY EVANS

'Maths is totally done differently to what I was teached when I was at school.'

DAVID BECKHAM

'The first 90 minutes of a football match are the most important.'

BOBBY ROBSON

'The Merseyside derby games are unique in the city.'

BRENDAN RODGERS

'The status quo remains the same.'

MICK MCCARTHY

'A win would be better than a draw.'

DENIS LAW

'I think I was 5ft 9in at birth.'

PETER CROUCH

'Ronaldo has got ten goals already, and I expect him to get into double figures.'

ANDY RITCHIE

'As with every young player, he's only eighteen.'

ALEX FERGUSON

'It was a fair decision, the penalty, even though it was debatable that it was inside or outside the box.'

BOBBY CHARLTON

'Burton really couldn't lose tonight. But they have.'

IAN WRIGHT

'Man City have got an extra man –
it seems like they've got fifteen players
on the pitch today.'

GARY NEVILLE

'It's 1–0 to United but they really should
be ahead.'

IAIN DOWIE

Trevor Sinclair: 'Forget the result, Leeds
have shown...'

Commentator: 'But, Trevor, the result is
everything. Leeds are minutes from defeat.'

***LEICESTER V LEEDS, MARCH 2022,* TALKSPORT**

'I've been booked fourteen times this
season. Eight were my fault but seven could
be disputed.'

GAZZA

'Me having no education. I had to
use my brains.'

BILL SHANKLY

'At least it was a victory – and at least
we won.'

BOBBY MOORE

'United may only get three or four chances
against you – but they can end up scoring
three, four or even five from them.'

CLARK CARLISLE

'We lost because we didn't win.'

BRAZILIAN RONALDO

'If you get to the edge of the penalty area with the ball and don't know what to do next, just stick the ball in the net. We can evaluate the other options later.'

BILL SHANKLY

'There's only a limited number of places in the top six.'

MICKY QUINN

'Nobody knows if Zidane is an angel or demon. He smiles like Saint Teresa and grimaces like a serial killer.'

ZIDANE ON ZIDANE

'I've got four words for you – Coppell for QPR. Hang on, that's not right. I'll check it... six words.'

RONNIE IRANI

'That is the 64-dollar question.'

LEIGHTON JAMES

'They must go for it now as they have nothing to lose but the match.'

RON ATKINSON

'In their last four, Blackburn have lost 3–0, 3–1, 5–3 and 3–2. It doesn't take a rocket scientist to work out that's 12 goals conceded.'

TALKSPORT'S ALAN BRAZIL

'5,000/1 weren't they (Leicester City) – but, in reality, they were 1,000,000/1 because it couldn't happen (winning the league).'

GARY LINEKER

'The champions are the team with the most points. If United have more points, it means they have more points, that's all. Nothing else.'

RAFA BENITEZ

'There's only one person gets you sacked – and that's the fans.'

PAUL MERSON

'Football boots are very technical and have lots of specific requirements.'

ZINEDINE ZIDANE

'In my time at Anfield we always said we had the best two teams on Merseyside – Liverpool and Liverpool reserves.'

BILL SHANKLY

MYSTIC MEG-SON AND CO

PREDICTIONS? DOH!

'Grimsby could drop out of the league and go into obliviation.'

RONNIE IRANI ON **TALKSPORT**

'You've got to believe you're going to win and I believe we'll win the World Cup – until the final whistle blows and we're knocked out.'

PETER SHILTON

'I can categorically tell you that Mario Balotelli will not be at Liverpool.'
(He ended up there)

BRENDAN RODGERS

'At this stage of the season, it's not just about improving, it's about getting better.'

RAY PARLOUR ON **TALKSPORT**

'Either side could win it, or it could
be a draw.'

RON ATKINSON

'I never make predictions – and I never will.'

GAZZA

'If Chelsea drop points, the cat's out in the
open. And you know what cats are like –
sometimes they don't come home.'

ALEX FERGUSON

'Whoever wins today will win the
championship, no matter who wins.'

DENIS LAW

'When you have a run of games where you keep winning and winning, you know it must end.'

RAFA BENITEZ

'My new tattoo is Jesus being carried by three cherubs. Obviously, the cherubs are my boys. At some point they are going to need to look after me. That's what they're doing in the picture. It means a lot.'

DAVID BECKHAM

'You must be joking. Do I look as if I'm a masochist ready to cut myself? How does relegation sound instead (for Liverpool)?'

ALEX FERGUSON

'Everybody has a different opinion in this league and nobody is a prophet. I personally don't know who will win the league. I managed 1,600 games so, if Nani knows (United will win it), he must be 1,600 times more intelligent than I am.'

ARSÈNE WENGER

'I'll probably have had enough of him (QPR captain Adel Taarabt) by Christmas, so hopefully he'll score 10 or 15 goals by then and get himself a move.'

NEIL WARNOCK

'When I heard the draw, I was out on the golf course. I had an eight-iron in one hand and my mobile in the other. When we came out with United, my club went further than the ball.'

HARRY REDKNAPP

'You never count your chickens before they hatch. I used to keep parakeets and I never counted every egg thinking I would get all eight birds. You just hoped they came out of the nest box looking all right. I'm like a swan at the moment. I look fine on top of the water – but under the water my little legs are going mad.'

IAN HOLLOWAY

'Jon Walters wanted to leave. We were four or five games into the season. He'd heard that Stoke were interested in him. I said: "Jon, I haven't had a call from anybody." He came back a few days later. "They're definitely after me." I said: "I've heard nothing. If there's a bid, I'll tell you. I've nothing to hide from you." "I'm not having this, he said." There was effing and blinding, a bit of shoving. "Why don't you f*****g believe me?" He was sold to Stoke a week later.'

ROY KEANE

'At the end of this game, the European Cup will be only six feet away from you, and you'll not even be able to touch it if we lose. And for many of you, that will be the closest you will ever get. Don't you dare come back in here without giving your all.'

ALEX FERGUSON AT HALF-TIME, 1999 EUROPEAN CUP FINAL

'The moral of the story is not to listen to those who tell you not to play the violin but stick to the tambourine.'

JOSÉ MOURINHO

'Clubs like ours won't be able to afford to go bananas in the transfer market. We can't get in ten Johan Elmanders because they're very expensive to buy and very expensive to run.'

BOLTON BOSS GARY MEGSON

'I bet him (Cristiano Ronaldo) he wouldn't get fifteen league goals and I'm going to have to change my bet with him. If he gets to fifteen I can change it and I am allowed to do that because I'm the manager. I'm going to make it a hundred and fifty now!'

ALEX FERGUSON

HOME IS WHERE THE ART IS

FOOTBALLING LIVES OFF THE PITCH

'I love pets, especially dogs.'

JÜRGEN KLOPP

'My foot, for a football player, is very beautiful!'

NEYMAR

'My family are really happy here at Liverpool and I am prepared to have my daughter with a Scouse accent – even though it is sometimes a problem for me.'

RAFA BENITEZ

'It's not a problem. In four or five days, I will be beautiful once again.'

INJURED CRISTIANO RONALDO

'Of course I didn't take my wife to see Rochdale as an anniversary present. It was her birthday and would I have got married during the football season? Anyway, it was Rochdale reserves.'

BILL SHANKLY

'I've always been in and out of fashion – mainly out, actually.'

PETER CROUCH

'I always used to go for blondes and quiet girls, but Victoria is the total opposite – dark and loud.'

DAVID BECKHAM

'Winning trophies has made me put on weight.'

RAFA BENITEZ

'Just to confirm to all my followers I have had a hair transplant. I was going bald at 25, why not.'

WAYNE ROONEY, TWITTER

'I'm not scared to spend money. If you go out with me one night, you will understand that.'

ARSÈNE WENGER

'I did a paper round as a kid, but the early mornings were too much. My dad took it over so I was getting paid fifteen quid a week, but he was doing it!'

PETER CROUCH

'I love Blackpool. We're very similar. We both look better in the dark.'

IAN HOLLOWAY

Reporter: 'Have you ever received death threats?'

Harry Redknapp: 'Only from the wife when I didn't do the washing up.'

'My ancestors were fighters, something I have inherited.'

ERIC CANTONA

'Come to my house and you'll find out if I'm gay. And bring your sister.'

ZLATAN IBRAHIMOVIĆ

'I enjoy being on holiday because you can do whatever you want – and people can't say anything to you.'

CRISTIANO RONALDO

'I'm not really that bothered by appearance. I know a few players who go off doing stuff in the mirror, ages before they go out to play a game, but I'm not really interested in that.'

WAYNE ROONEY

'My favourite movie is *The Lion King*, the original one – for kids.'

BRUNO FERNANDES

'Some men over-tweeze their eyebrows, and it's just too perfect. Men are meant to have kind of a bushy brow. Too much aftershave is also off-putting – it's one of my pet hates.'

DAVID BECKHAM

'If I'm staying in a hotel or sleeping on my own, I have the hairdryer on.'

WAYNE ROONEY

45

'When it comes to being bad ass nothing beats this (being a footballer). It took me 17 years and 114 days to become an overnight success.'

LIONEL MESSI

'If someone is too perfect they won't look good. Imperfection is important.'

ERIC CANTONA

'I've heard some of Victoria's new album and it's frightening.'

DAVID BECKHAM

'I don't normally cook. But if I did, it would be beans, sausage, bacon and eggs. I never really get to eat that, to be honest.'

WAYNE ROONEY

'I still remember when my teacher told
me that football wouldn't give me
anything to eat.'

CRISTIANO RONALDO

'I listen to 50 Cent, Jay-Z, Stereophonics,
Arctic Monkeys and the musical, *Oliver!*
I can sing every tune.'

WAYNE ROONEY

'My wife doesn't like football. One day
she called me ten minutes before a game to
find out where I was.'

PETER CROUCH

'Now I'm better behaved. You get older,
more responsible and quieter. But if I want
to dye my hair red or blue, I'll dye it.'

NEYMAR

'Tom Cruise – he's a lot more famous
than me.'

DAVID BECKHAM

'I've had some proud moments in my career
but finishing second in the dads' race was
special.'

PETER CROUCH

'I like nice clothes, whether they're
dodgy or not.'

DAVID BECKHAM

'I can't live without posting pictures.'

NEYMAR

'I love Barbados – it's really relaxing.'

WAYNE ROONEY

'People whistle at me because I am good-looking, rich and a great footballer.
They are jealous.'

CRISTIANO RONALDO

'My parents have been there for me, ever since I was about seven.'

DAVID BECKHAM

Journalist: 'If you hadn't become a professional footballer, what would you have been?' Peter Crouch: 'A virgin.'

'The kid (Cristiano Ronaldo) makes you sick. He looks the part, he walks the part, he is the part. He is six-foot something, fit as a flea and good-looking. Surely he's got something wrong with him? Hopefully he'll be hung like a hamster.'

IAN HOLLOWAY

STANDS AND DELIVER

ON THE FANS – AND FROM THEM

'Spurs fans are feeling very boyish about the future.'

ALAN BRAZIL ON TALKSPORT

'He wanted to know where I was. My wife told him I was doing a press conference and I'd be back soon. So Sean Bean started swearing at her and my five-year-old son. It's your f****** husband who got us relegated, he's a f****** w*****. That's Sean Bean, the tough guy actor. Some kind of tough guy, hey – reducing a five-year-old kid and his mum to tears.'

NEIL WARNOCK

'Nice to see your own fans boo you. That's what loyal support is.'

WAYNE ROONEY

'I'm so proud that the fans still sing my name, but I fear tomorrow they will stop. I fear it because I love it. And everything you love, you fear you will lose.'

ERIC CANTONA

'When I was in charge at Porto, we played in the UEFA Cup final against a Scottish side – Celtic. I've never seen such emotional people. It was unbelievable.'

JOSÉ MOURINHO

'Away from home our fans (Man United) are fantastic, I'd call them the hardcore fans. But at home they have a few drinks and probably the prawn sandwiches and they don't realise what's going on out on the pitch.'

ROY KEANE

'You can change your wife, your politics, your religion – but never, never can you change your favourite football team.'

ERIC CANTONA

'If I had wanted to be protected in a quiet job, I could have stayed at Porto. I would have been second, after God, in the eyes of the fans even if I had never won another thing.'

JOSÉ MOURINHO

'My best moment? I have a lot of good moments – but the one I prefer is when I kicked the hooligan.'

ERIC CANTONA

And fans have always insisted on a right to reply, with witty terrace chants:

'Chairs from IKEA/You got your chairs from IKEA!'

BIRMINGHAM FANS TO BRISTOL CITY

'Beaten by a franchise, you're getting beaten by a franchise.'

MK DONS FANS TO BARNET SUPPORTERS

'His name is Rio and he watches from the stand.'

WEST HAM FANS TO THE TUNE OF DURAN DURAN'S 'RIO' WHEN RIO FERDINAND WAS BANNED FOR MISSING A DRUGS TEST

Or the Man United faithful's version:

'His name is Rio and he dances on the grass/Don't take the ball from him, he'll kick your f****** ass.'

'He's fast, he's red, he talks like Father Ted, Robbie Keane.'

LIVERPOOL FANS ON THEIR IRISH NUMBER 7, ROBBIE KEANE

'John Carew, Carew. He likes a lap dance or two. He might even pay for you. John Carew, Carew.'

ASTON VILLA FANS TO THE TUNE OF 'QUE SERA SERA' AFTER IT WAS WRONGLY CLAIMED THE NORWEGIAN FRONTMAN WENT TO A STRIP CLUB

'You only live round the corner.'

***FULHAM FANS TAUNT MAN UNITED SUPPORTERS
AT CRAVEN COTTAGE***

'He's red, he's sound, he's banned from
every ground, Carra's dad, Carra's dad.'

***LIVERPOOL FANS ABOUT JAMIE CARRAGHER'S
FATHER, WHO WAS ACCUSED OF BEING DRUNK
AT A FOOTBALL MATCH***

'You're shish, and you know you are.'

***CHELSEA FANS' WITTY CHANT WHEN TURKS
GALATASARAY PLAYED AT STAMFORD BRIDGE***

'He's bald, he's red, he sleeps in Fergie's bed
– Howard Webb, Howard Webb.'

***LIVERPOOL FANS HAVE A GO AT REF
HOWARD WEBB FOR HIS ALLEGED BIAS
TOWARDS MAN UNITED***

'Your teeth are offside, your teeth are offside, Luis Suárez, your teeth are offside.'

UNITED FANS HIT BACK WITH A DITTY ABOUT LIVERPOOL'S LUIS SUÁREZ

'He's big, he's red, his feet stick out the bed, Peter Crouch, Peter Crouch.'

THE KOP SERENADE THEIR BIG CENTRE-FORWARD

SIMPLY THE BEAST

TRAINING TIPS AND FAILS

'If you train badly, you play badly. If you work like a beast in training, you play the same way.'

PEP GUARDIOLA

'If you think about it, running forms a large part of training and playing for any footballer.'

DEAN ASHTON

'We won't be able to shut him up when he (Jimmy Bullard) comes back to us (for training, from his England call-up). But then again, there's no change there.'

RAY LEWINGTON

'Train the right way. Help each other. It's a form of socialism without the politics.'

BILL SHANKLY

Brendan's chihuahua doesn't do that. During the week it sleeps, eats and trains a little bit. So I have to say his chihuahua is a privileged one.

JOSÉ MOURINHO, ON BRENDAN RODGERS' PET

'I miss Manchester, especially the apple crumble and custard they served at Carrington after training.'

CRISTIANO RONALDO

'I'm lucky, I never had to watch my weight. In the summer I go off, don't do much in the way of exercise, eat what I like, come back exactly the same weight. Which p***es off a few, I can tell you. The way Charlie Adam looks at me.'

PETER CROUCH

'Come and see my coaching certificates – they are called the European Cup and league championships.'

BRIAN CLOUGH

'I can't keep protecting people who don't want to run about and train, who are 3 stone overweight. What am I supposed to keep saying? "Keep getting your 60, 70 grand a week but don't train?" What's the game coming to?'

HARRY REDKNAPP

'I remember once when I got to training the day after a loss, I was still so angry and went into the changing room with Michael Carrick. We found Jesse Lingard and Paul Pogba dancing to music.'

WAYNE ROONEY ON TWITTER

'My old trainer used to tell us not to blast, but to caress the ball whenever we took possession. If the ball were a woman, she'd be spending all night with Berbatov.'

IAN HOLLOWAY

Pablo Couñago was a player I didn't particularly like or get on with. No club was interested in taking him – and I was happy to tell him that. I just found him dead lazy. He went: 'How are we going to win anything with you as manager?' I nearly physically attacked him – but I didn't.

ROY KEANE

'If Roman Abramovich helped me out in training, we would be bottom of the league and if I had to work in his world of big business, we would be bankrupt.'

JOSÉ MOURINHO

'After his first training session in Heaven, George Best, from his favourite right wing, turned the head of God who was filling in at left-back. I would love him to save me a place in his team – George Best that is, not God.'

ERIC CANTONA

'I've found myself on some days leaving home at three in the morning. I'm outside the training ground at five, but they don't open up until seven. I'm just sitting there, listening to the radio.'

HARRY REDKNAPP

'I think in England you eat too much sugar and meat and not enough vegetables.'

ARSÈNE WENGER

'It's a 90-minute game, for sure. In fact, I used to train for a 180-minute game so that when the whistle blew at the end of the match, I could have played another 90 minutes.'

BILL SHANKLY

SH*T AND YOU
KNOW YOU ARE

TALENT AND MEDIOCRITY

'Sam Allardyce should learn a bit of humidity.'

JOHNNY GILES

'I know how it goes. Six or seven months ago, I was the Manager of the Year and was going to be this and that, tactically this and tactically that. But now, because we have lost two world-class players, I am useless. But I accept that.'

BRENDAN RODGERS

'(Distraught) Alex McLeish has just had his hands in his head.'

CHRIS KAMARA

'Nottingham Forest are having a bad run, they've lost six matches in a row now without winning.'

COMMENTATOR DAVID COLEMAN

It was Tottenham at home. I thought: 'Please don't go on about Tottenham, we all know what Tottenham are about. They are nice and tidy but we'll f*****g do them.' Then Alex (Ferguson) came in and said, 'Lads, it's only Tottenham.' And that was it! Brilliant!

ROY KEANE

'He (Sam Allardyce) will be getting a hug and a kiss from me – maybe even two!'

ALEX FERGUSON AFTER BOLTON
BEAT CHELSEA

'He (Jose Mourinho) is out of order, disconnected with reality and disrespectful. When you give success to stupid people, it makes them more stupid sometimes and not more intelligent.'

ARSÈNE WENGER

'I used to have a saying that when a player is at his peak, he feels as though he can climb Everest in his slippers. That's what he (Paul Ince) was like.'

ALEX FERGUSON

'With all the stones being thrown against me, you could build a monument.'

JOSÉ MOURINHO

'If you eat caviar every day, it's difficult to return to sausages.'

ARSÈNE WENGER AFTER BEING BOOED BY HIS OWN FANS

'The problem with you, Son, is that all your brains are in your head.'

BILL SHANKLY

'An artist in my eyes, is someone who can lighten up a dark room. I have never and will never find a difference between the pass from Pelé to Carlos Alberto in the final of the World Cup in 1970 and the poetry of the young Rimbaud, who stretches chords from steeple to steeple and garlands from window to window. There is in each of these human manifestations an expression of beauty which touches us and gives us a feeling of eternity.'

ERIC CANTONA

'When John Lennon got assassinated, the joke was that if I'd have shot him, he'd still be alive today.'

GARRY BIRTLES

OFF THE WALL

SURPRISES AND IDIOSYNCRASIES

'I'm not surprised, but it is surprising.'

GLENN HODDLE

'It's not easy when someone pulls your ponytail.'

DAVID BECKHAM INTERVIEW,
INDEPENDENT

'We were the only team who got fined if we didn't go out on a Friday night, it was one of those things you did in those days. We would have won four European Cups if we hadn't been drinking, I tell you.'

GARRY BIRTLES ON BRIAN CLOUGH'S
MANAGEMENT

'I'd like to play for an Italian club, like Barcelona.'

MARK DRAPER

'I've got more respect for (Alex) Ferguson than anyone else in the game. He's like a Scouser, really. He's funny, doesn't mind telling people to f*** off, and he even votes Labour. I love him.'

JAMIE CARRAGHER, BBC SPORT, 2008

'I always wanted to be a hairdresser.'

DAVID BECKHAM

'I am not the first player to have sworn on TV and I won't be the last.'

WAYNE ROONEY

'It was a freakish incident. If I tried it 100 or a million times it couldn't happen again. If I could, I would have carried on playing!'

ALEX FERGUSON ON KICKING A BOOT INTO BECKHAM'S FACE

'I was only four or five days in driving my new Aston Martin. I was a little bit embarrassed, I didn't feel comfortable in it. I was driving through Cheshire and pulled up at some lights alongside Roy Keane. He looked at me like I was something on the bottom of his shoe. I had shades on, was listening to garage music, and thinking I was the man. He firmly let me know I wasn't the man. As he sped off, I looked at myself in the mirror and I sold the car that week. I took about a 20 grand hit on it.'

PETER CROUCH

'I have got this obsessive compulsive disorder where I have to have everything in a straight line, or everything has to be in pairs.'

DAVID BECKHAM

'If we're on long-haul flights, I've been known to sleep on the floor so I hear the engine.'

WAYNE ROONEY

'We've been asked to do *Playboy* together, me and Victoria, as a pair. I don't think I'll ever go naked, but I'll never say never.'

DAVID BECKHAM

'Sometimes you look in a field and you see a cow and you think it's a better cow than the one you've got in the field.'

ALEX FERGUSON ON ROONEY'S DECISION NOT TO LEAVE UNITED AFTER ALL

'I would rather play with ten men than wait for a player who is late for the bus.'

JOSÉ MOURINHO

'They must know somebody at the Football
League, Norwich, getting their fixtures
like they have. Poor old Dave Jones
(at Cardiff) was moaning about it the other
day. I think Delia Smith must be cooking
something for them.'

IAN HOLLOWAY

'I don't see the problem with footballers
taking their shirts off after scoring a goal.
They enjoy it and the young ladies enjoy
it too. I suppose that's one of the main
reasons women come to football games – to
see the young men take their shirts off. Of
course, they'd have to go and watch another
game because my lads are as ugly as sin.'

IAN HOLLOWAY

'It's good to get angry. It's an emotion and part of the game. It's good to go a bit mad but I don't throw teacups around. That's not my style – I'd rather throw punches.'

ROY KEANE

Hajduk Split defender Goran Granić was criticised by fans for no longer going in hard on opponents. The Croatian explained it was because had found God, adding, 'I'm so devoted to God now that I have started to avoid committing fouls during matches. God has created football for fun and relaxation. He would not like players to commit harsh fouls.'

Sheffield United players said their run of good results in 2003 was down to eating Cow & Gate Chocolate Rice Sandwiches before matches. Cow & Gate cashed in on the publicity by sending them freebies of their baby food product.

ALLEGATIONS AND ALLIGATORS

TENSIONS ON AND OFF THE PITCH

'Allegations (in the dressing room) are all very well, but I would like to know who these alligators are.'

RON SAUNDERS

'The tension is palatable.'

MATT JACKSON

'You might as well talk to my baby daughter. You'll get more sense out of her (than Alex Ferguson).'

KENNY DALGLISH

'If you don't know the answer to that question, then I think you are an ostrich. Your head must be in the sand. Are you flexible enough to get your head in the sand? My suspicion would be no. I can. You can't (to a journalist).'

NIGEL PEARSON

'My first game for Celtic was Clyde, away...
we lost 2–1, it was a nightmare. After the
game – the disappointment. As I was taking
my jersey off, I noticed the Nike tag was still
on it. When I got on the bus John Hartson,
a really good guy, was already sitting there
and he was eating a packet of crisps – with
a fizzy drink. I said to myself, Welcome to
Hell.'

ROY KEANE

'I play with passion and fire. I have to accept
that sometimes this fire does harm.'

ERIC CANTONA

'My heart was in my hands.'

RICKY SBRAGIA

'I have no doubt El Hadji Diouf will be here next season, but he's finished for this one.'

SAM ALLARDYCE

'Tense and nervous are not the words, though they are the words.'

CHRIS KAMARA

'If you have a car and you win a race, you cannot just settle for that. You must try and make the car better. We're a good car (Newcastle United) but you always want a bigger engine (more transfer cash).'

RAFA BENITEZ

'It's getting tickly now – squeaky-bum time, I call it.'

ALEX FERGUSON

'It's like being on the *Titanic* and seeing there's only one lifeboat left (to avoid relegation).'

HARRY REDKNAPP

'Pardew has come out and criticised me. He is the worst at haranguing referees. He shoves them and makes a joke of it. How he can criticise me is unbelievable. He forgets the help I gave him, by the way. The press have had a field day. The only person they have not spoken to is Barack Obama because he is busy. It is unfortunate, but I am the manager of the most famous club in the world. Not Newcastle, a wee club in the North-East.'

ALEX FERGUSON

'Our first session (at Ipswich) was open to the fans. But nobody came. Then there was the blue training kit. I don't like f*****g blue. City were blue. Rangers were blue. My biggest rivals were blue. Is that childish? I couldn't feel it – the chemistry.'

ROY KEANE

'I'm no f*****g talking to you (the press). He's a f*****g great player (Juan Sebastián Verón). Yous are f*****g idiots.'

ALEX FERGUSON

'It's wrong the league programme is extended so United can rest up and win everything.'

ARSÈNE WENGER

'The amount of fights I've had in Cork would probably be another book. I mean, people go on about my problems off the field, but they don't even know the half of it.'

ROY KEANE

'For the people that I love I only have one face – but for some people we can't have one face.'

IAN HOLLOWAY

'When I was about sixteen, I got my ball taken off me by the police for playing in the street, which is pathetic really.'

WAYNE ROONEY

'Spurs... Spursy! How many times do we have to say it? Whatever's in that club's DNA – the players – there's a weakness there. It's really pathetic, but I wasn't surprised. Going up to Middlesbrough in midweek, probably a bit cold. No surprises there.'

ROY KEANE ON ITV

Sir Alex Ferguson celebrated his horse Clan Des Obeaux claiming victory in the Betway Bowl at Aintree in April 2022, in typical feisty Fergie style. When asked what the triumph meant to him, the ex-Man United boss couldn't resist a dig at old enemy Liverpool, saying, 'We're delighted. It's always good to win on Merseyside!'

Liverpool manager Bill Shankly tried to convince his team they had nothing to fear from Man United, dismissing the ability of eight of their players. But Kop skipper Emlyn Hughes moaned, 'That's all very well, boss, but you haven't said anything about George Best, Bobby Charlton or Denis Law.' Shankly growled back, 'Are you trying to tell me that you can't beat a team that's only got three players in it?'

THE BIG BAD WOLVES

FOOTBALLING RIVALRIES

'If Chelsea are naive and pure, then I'm Little Red Riding Hood.'

RAFA BENITEZ

'My advice for Sebastian Kehl (Borussia Dortmund captain) is this... if you have a 35-point deficit in the league, it is better to shut up.'

PEP GUARDIOLA (WHEN BAYERN MUNICH BOSS)

'I do not exchange my shirt with assassins.'

CRISTIANO RONALDO AFTER PORTUGAL V ISRAEL, 2014

'When I've got nothing better to do, I look down the league table to see how Everton are getting along.'

BILL SHANKLY

87

'There has been a lot of expectation on Manchester City and with the spending they have done they have to win something. Sometimes you have a noisy neighbour and have to live with it. You can't do anything about them.'

SIR ALEX FERGUSON

'Everyone thinks they have the prettiest wife at home.'

ARSÈNE WENGER HITS BACK AT ALEX FERGUSON'S ARSENAL PUTDOWN

'People say I'm hard, I'm Mr Angry. I'm this, I'm that. I just want to win matches. There's no point going out there and being Mr Nice Guy. We get 55,000 at Old Trafford and I don't think they want fellas going out there and thinking: Ah, if we lose, so what?'

ROY KEANE

'He's a lucky guy, Cristiano, he always gets
first row tickets to see Messi win
the awards.'

ZLATAN IBRAHIMOVIĆ

'The reality is he (Arsène Wenger) is a
specialist because eight years without a
piece of silverware – that is failure.'

JOSÉ MOURINHO

'The difference between Everton and the
Queen Mary is that Everton carry more
passengers.'

BILL SHANKLY

'You would think I was guilty of committing
more crimes than Osama bin Laden.'

NEIL WARNOCK

'Ferguson never turned up. I thought that was out of order. He called me a few days later to apologise. He said he'd had to rush off after the game and he'd waited a long time for me. I told him he should have a drink with me, like he would have with any other manager, and that he hadn't shown me nor my staff proper respect.'

ROY KEANE

'Ferguson does what he wants and you (reporters) are all down at his feet. He doesn't interest me and doesn't matter to me at all. I will never answer to any provocation from him anymore.'

ARSÈNE WENGER

'All they (Manchester City) can talk about is Manchester United.'

ALEX FERGUSON

'There is one thing you must know about Marko Arnautović if you want to understand what makes him tick – he believes he's the best player in the world.'

PETER CROUCH

'Have Tottenham closed the gap on Arsenal? Last time I checked, they were still four miles and eleven titles away.'

ARSÈNE WENGER

'I studied Italian five hours a day for many months to ensure I could communicate with the players, media and fans. Ranieri had been in England for five years and still struggled to say 'good morning' and 'good afternoon'.

JOSÉ MOURINHO, GOAL.COM

'The two managers I really dislike are Stan Ternent and Gary Megson. The old saying that I wouldn't p**s on them if they were on fire applies.'

NEIL WARNOCK

'Roy Keane's like a shark. He has those eyes. You don't know if he is going to buy you a drink or eat you.'

IAN HOLLOWAY

'Will those on telly yesterday be remembered for what they've achieved? None whatsoever. I wouldn't trust them to walk my dog. There are ex-players and ex-referees being given airtime who I wouldn't listen to in a pub.'

ROY KEANE (BEFORE HE BECAME A TV PUNDIT)

This is football from the nineteenth century. It's very difficult to play a football match when only one team wants to play. A football match is about two teams playing. I told Big Sam (Allardyce), they need points. To come here the way they (West Ham) did, is that acceptable? Maybe it is, they need points. The only thing I could bring more was Black & Decker – a Black & Decker to destroy the West Ham wall.'

JOSÉ MOURINHO

'Some (Roy Hodgson) can't see a priest on a mountain of sugar.'

RAFA BENITEZ

MERMAIDS AND OTHER MYTHS

MANAGERS IN AT THE DEEP END

'Managing a league club is like making love
to a mermaid... you should always be aiming
for a top-half finish.'

IAN HOLLOWAY

'As a manager, you are important
sometimes, and you make mistakes, but
the most important people are your
staff and your players. Never call me
'The Special One!'

RAFA BENITEZ

'If it doesn't go right tonight, Wenger
has another leg up his sleeve.'

GLENN HODDLE

'Certain people are for me, and certain
people are pro me.'

TERRY VENABLES

'That sort of stuff, we're bigger than that.
When you do that with footballers like he
(Alex Ferguson) said about Leeds and when
you do things like that about a man like
Stuart Pearce, I've kept really quiet, but he
really went down in my estimation when
he said that, we have not resorted to that.
But I'll tell him, you can tell him, he'll be
watching. We're still fighting for this title,
and he's got to go to Middlesbrough and
get something and I'll tell you, honestly, I will
love it if we beat them. LOVE IT!'

KEVIN KEEGAN

'Myths grow all the time. If I was to listen
to the number of times I've thrown teacups,
then we've gone through some crockery
in this place.'

ALEX FERGUSON

'Sir Alex has a special place in my life. In fact, he was the main man. I was not famous, I was not a star. I arrived at Old Trafford as just another young talent. He was the one who told me to do all the right things. He gave me the opportunity to play in one of the biggest clubs in the world. So he is one of the most important people in the world for me. I worked with Sir Alex for a few years and I know he deserves everything that he has achieved in his career. He works so hard, he is clever, he has experience, he is a human guy.'

CRISTIANO RONALDO, **DAILY MIRROR**

'I needed two stitches after Alex (Ferguson) kicked the boot at me.'

DAVID BECKHAM

'Arsène Wenger asked me to have a trial with Arsenal when I was seventeen. I turned it down. Zlatan doesn't do auditions.'

ZLATAN IBRAHIMOVIĆ

'I am prepared. The more pressure there is, the stronger I am. In Portugal, we say the bigger the ship, the stronger the storm. Fortunately for me, I have always been in big ships. FC Porto was a very big ship in Portugal, Chelsea was also a big ship in England and Inter was a great ship in Italy. Now I'm at Real Madrid, which is considered the biggest ship on the planet.'

JOSÉ MOURINHO

'My wife will be glad about Mourinho coming to Bramall Lane because he's a good-looking swine, isn't he?'

NEIL WARNOCK

'We've got sports scientists who insist it's important for the lads to eat after games to refuel, even if it's 2am. I used to refuel after games at West Ham until half past three in the morning in a different way, but I'm old school.'

HARRY REDKNAPP

'If I wanted to have an easy job, working with the big protection of what I have already done before, I would have stayed at Porto – beautiful blue chair, the UEFA Champions League trophy, God, and after God, me.'

***JOSÉ MOURINHO*, GUARDIAN**

'Cloughie was dead right (to punch him), absolutely. It was the best thing he ever did for me.'

ROY KEANE

José Mourinho is a big star. He's nice. The
first time he met (Zlatan's wife) Helena, he
whispered to her: 'Helena, you have only
one mission – feed Zlatan, let him sleep,
keep him happy.' That guy says whatever
he wants. I like him.

ZLATAN IBRAHIMOVIĆ

'Alex Ferguson is the best manager I've ever
had at this level. Well, he's the only manager
I've actually had at this level. But he's the
best manager I've ever had.'

DAVID BECKHAM

'They say he's an intelligent man, right
(Wenger)? Speaks five languages! I've got
a fifteen-year-old boy from the Ivory Coast
who speaks five languages.'

ALEX FERGUSON

100

'I had always known Stan Ternent was a d***head. But when Sheffield United played Burnley in 2001, he behaved like a deranged lunatic. I'd told my assistant Kevin Blackwell to keep an eye on Ternent. I knew he'd be trying to put pressure on the ref. So when Ternent came round the corner, frothing at the mouth, Blackie told him to leave it out. That was all the encouragement Ternent needed. He launched himself at Blackie and butted him. Blackwell swung a right hook and smacked him on the nose. He sploshed him good and proper. In Ternent's autobiography he tells how he gave Blackwell a good hiding. But we saw the incident differently. Blackie had a little cut on his lip. Ternent was in bits.'

NEIL WARNOCK, IN HIS AUTOBIOGRAPHY

The last song before the players went on to the pitch was 'Dancing Queen' by Abba. What really worried me was that none of the players, not one, said: 'Get that s*** off.' They were going out to play a match, men versus men, testosterone levels were high. You've got to hit people at pace. F*****g 'Dancing Queen'. It worried me. I didn't have as many leaders as I thought.

ROY KEANE

'I was surprised by what has been said, but maybe they (Manchester United) are nervous because we are at the top of the table. But I want to talk about facts. I want to be clear, I do not want to play mind games too early, although they seem to want to start. But I have seen some facts... You can analyse the facts and come to your own decision and ideas.'

RAFA BENITEZ

Rodney Marsh was picked to play for England in a 1973 World Cup qualifier against Wales, but boss Alf Ramsey had his misgivings about the maverick Manchester City striker. Before the match, Alf warned him: 'Marsh, if you don't work hard, I'm going to pull you off at half-time.' Quick as a flash, Rodney quipped: 'Blimey, boss! At Man City, all we get is a cup of tea and an orange!' Ramsey didn't enjoy the joke and it would prove to be the last of Rodney's nine international caps.

ON THE TRANSFER TRAIL

MISS WORLD AND A LOO-NY LOCK-IN

'Michael Owen could be Sir Alex's best-ever buy, even though he didn't buy him.'

GLENN HODDLE

I got Robbie's (Savage) mobile number and rang him. It went to his voicemail: 'Hi, it's Robbie, whazzup!' Like the Budweiser ad. I never called him back. I thought: 'I can't be f*****g signing that.'

ROY KEANE

'The story of me being locked in the toilet by Tiago is true. It's a shame it got out, as this was something I told a friend in confidence. In any case, Alessandro Del Piero responded to the noise of me punching the door and offered to break it down.'

JUVENTUS PRESIDENT GIOVANNI COBOLLI GIGLI ON THE PORTUGUESE PLAYER'S REACTION TO POTENTIAL SALE TO EVERTON

'It's like you wanting to marry Miss World and she doesn't want you – what can I do about it? I can try to help you, but if she does not want to marry you, what can I do?'

ARSÈNE WENGER'S UPSET THAT JOSE ANTONIO REYES WANTS TO LEAVE

'I've never wanted to leave. I'm here for the rest of my life and hopefully after that.'

ALAN SHEARER

'All that remains is for a few dots and commas to be crossed.'

MITCHELL THOMAS

'We have sold Robinho for reasons of human nature. The fact is we have accepted an offer from Manchester City and that he is not going for sporting reasons.'

REAL MADRID PRESIDENT RAMÓN CALDERÓN

106

'Ronaldo has said he wants to play for the biggest club in the world, so we will see in January if he is serious.'

SULAIMAN AL-FAHIM, OF MAN CITY'S NEW ABU DHABI OWNERS

'It's disappointing, but I'll get over it. He (Lee McCulloch) says it's for family reasons he wants to go back to Scotland – but he forgot to put that in his transfer request! Whoever wrote it has not quite got the wording right!'

PAUL JEWELL, FORMER WIGAN BOSS

'It is a big surprise to me because he (Sol Campbell) cancelled his contract to go abroad. Have you sold Portsmouth to a foreign country?'

ARSÈNE WENGER

'When you buy me, you are buying a Ferrari. If you drive a Ferrari you put premium fuel in the tank, you drive onto the motorway and you floor the accelerator. Guardiola filled up with diesel and went for a spin in the countryside. If that's what he wanted, he should have bought himself a Fiat from the start.'

ZLATAN IBRAHIMOVIĆ

'One day in 1959, when Huddersfield were playing Cardiff City, Tom Williams, who was then chairman of Liverpool, and Harry Latham, a director, came down the slope at Leeds Road to see me. Mr Williams said: 'How would you like to manage the best club in the country?' 'Why,' I asked, 'is Matt Busby packing it in?'

BILL SHANKLY

'When a club is interested in you, the manager generally sells it to you. 'Listen, we'd love to have you here.' But I met Gordon Strachan, the Celtic manager, in London – and he told me, 'I'm not really worried if you sign for us or not. We're okay without you.' So I said to myself, 'F**k him, I'm signing!' I think it was one of the reasons I signed for them – to prove Gordon wrong.'

ROY KEANE

Manchester United were once so skint, they signed a player for two fridge freezers. It happened in 1927 when assistant manager – and ice cream business owner – Louis Rocca used two of his freezers to snap up Stockport County's Hugh McLenahan. Rocca even filled them with ice cream as a gesture of goodwill.

Fourth Division Romanian team Regal
Hornia were delighted when Second
Division side UTA Arad agreed to sell them
defender Marius Cioara for 30lbs of pork
sausages. Unfortunately for Regal, he then
retired a day later, saying he wouldn't be
able to face fans' taunts about the fee.

THE SACK RACE

**RASH CREAM, BREKKIE AND
A COLD LAKE**

'The only decisions I'm making at the moment are whether I have tea, coffee, toast or cornflakes in the morning.'

SAM ALLARDYCE AFTER HE WAS DISMISSED AT NEWCASTLE

'I left United, but my heart didn't.'

DAVID BECKHAM

'I am more than happy at Blackpool and I am afraid the chairman will need a hell of a tub of cream to get rid of me. I'm like a bad rash and not easily curable.'

IAN HOLLOWAY

'Will Bielsa and his translator both be looking down as they say goodbye?'

COMMENTATOR SAM MATTERFACE ON MARCELO'S SACKING AS LEEDS BOSS

'If (Ralf) Rangnick is a cold shower for (Man) United's players, (Diego) Simeone would be like being thrown into a freezing cold lake.'

EUROPEAN FOOTBALL EXPERT ANDY BRASSELL ON RUMOURS THAT THE ATLÉTICO MADRID BOSS MAY TAKE OVER AT OLD TRAFFORD

'My greatest mistake? I once took a three-day maternity leave. I had my daughter on a Wednesday, and then went back to the office on the Monday to sack a manager.'

KARREN BRADY

'When you're younger, you worry about the sack and getting abuse and things, but when you get to my age, you become less bothered about those things. It becomes more like a hobby.'

NEIL WARNOCK

'I went into a club who were sitting dead last in League Two, then I got them out of the relegation zone within ten games, only to then get the sack... I don't get it.'

HARRY KEWELL

'At a football club, there's a holy trinity – the players, the manager and the supporters. Directors don't come into it. They are only there to sign the cheques.'

BILL SHANKLY

'If I were Niall Quinn, I'd try to get someone in ESP.'

ALAN BRAZIL, TALKSPORT

'What are they going to do, shoot me? It's not war, you know.'

HARRY REDKNAPP

Former West Ham striker Leroy Rosenior was appointed boss of struggling Torquay in 2007 – and claimed he was sacked after ten minutes, breaking the record for English football's shortest managerial reign.

THE SPECIAL ONES

LEGENDS IN THEIR OWN
LUNCHTIMES

'When I think I've made an error, it can cause me a sleepless night. But that only happens rarely.'

LOUIS VAN GAAL

'I'm not suited to Bolton or Blackburn, I would be more suited to Inter Milan or Real Madrid. It wouldn't be a problem to me to go and manage those clubs because I would win the double or the league every time. Give me Manchester United or Chelsea and I would do the same, it wouldn't be a problem.'

SAM ALLARDYCE

'People in football love to talk about mental strength. Well, I'm the strongest dude you're ever going to meet.'

ROMELU LUKAKU

'No one did what I did last season and for this, I deserve the Golden Boot and why not the best World Player award?'

CRISTIANO RONALDO

'We usually say that you cannot become a legend before death. But I am a living legend.'

ZLATAN IBRAHIMOVIĆ

'When people are talking about you, it means that you exist.'

ERIC CANTONA

'Zidane was from another planet. When Zidane stepped onto the pitch, the ten other guys just got suddenly better. It is that simple.'

ZINEDINE ZIDANE

'I was the best manager in Britain because I was never devious or cheated anyone. I'd break my wife's legs if I played against her, but I'd never cheat her.'

BILL SHANKLY

'My biggest mentor is myself because I've had to study, so that's been my biggest influence.'

BRENDAN RODGERS

'I'm thinking of opening the Brian Clough Academy of Management. It couldn't fail – they'd be queueing overnight.'

BRIAN CLOUGH

'I am José Mourinho and I don't change. I arrive (at Real Madrid) with all my qualities and my defects.'

MOURINHO, CNN.COM

'I am who I am: confident, arrogant, dominant, honest, hard-working and innovative.'

LOUIS VAN GAAL

'Neymar is massively overrated.'

NEYMAR

'I am like wine. The older I get, the better I get.'

ZLATAN IBRAHIMOVIĆ

'Please don't say I'm arrogant, because what I say is true. I am European champion, so I'm not one out of the bottle. I think I'm a special one.'

JOSÉ MOURINHO

'Zidane is probably the best player there has been in the past twenty years. France have recovered the best Zidane and they have progressively grown throughout this tournament.'

ZINEDINE ZIDANE

'Who's been the biggest single influence on my career? That's easy. Me.'

BRIAN CLOUGH

'It bugs me when I see other managers getting top jobs and I know they're not as good as me.'

NEIL WARNOCK

'The River Trent is lovely. I know, because I've walked on it for eighteen years.'

BRIAN CLOUGH

'He (Paul Scholes) was a top, top player. But I still don't fall for the boy-next-door image, or that he's dead humble. He has more of an edge to him. Everyone thinks he lives in a council flat. The Class of 92 are all good players, but their role at the club has become exaggerated. 'Class of 92' seems to have grown its own legs, it has become a brand. It's as if they were a team away from the team, and they're not shy of plugging into it. We all had the same aims. We all had the hunger.'

ROY KEANE

'You don't have to love me. You don't even have to like me, but you will respect me.'

JOSÉ MOURINHO

'I won't ever be going to a top-four club because I'm not called Allardici, just Allardyce.'

SAM ALLARDYCE

An interviewer tried to show off how well read he was when quizzing keeper David James: 'French author Albert Camus, a fellow goalkeeper, once wrote, "One sentence will suffice for the modern man: He fornicated and read the papers." Doesn't that describe modern football? Shagging birds and then reading about it?' James replied: 'No, I don't read the paper.'

TACTICAL GENIUSES (OR NOT)

BAZOOKAS AND BURGLARS

'Playing with wingers is more effective against European sides like Brazil, than English sides like Wales.'

RON GREENWOOD, FORMER ENGLAND MANAGER

'Tackling is a dying heart.'

CHRIS KAMARA

'It rankles with me at times that I have to remind people what I have done. You have to accept it for what it is. If you start talking about it too much, you just get labelled big-headed. But if no one else is going to talk about it, you have to talk about it. The lingering long-ball s***, the old style, all that rubbish – that's never been me and never been a part of what I am.'

SAM ALLARDYCE

'There's a little triangle... five left-footed players.'

RON ATKINSON

'We have a bow and arrow and if we aim well, we can hit the target. The problem is that Bayern has a bazooka. The probability that they will hit the target is clearly higher.'

JÜRGEN KLOPP

'I've got the passion but no idea of tactics – I'd be like a black Kevin Keegan.'

IAN WRIGHT

'If you're a burglar, it's no good waiting about outside somebody's house, looking good with your swag bag ready. Just get in there, burgle them and come out. I don't advocate that obviously, it's just an analogy.'

IAN HOLLOWAY

'My free-kick secret? I just look at the net and say take the kick, Cristiano.'

CRISTIANO RONALDO

'Football is a game based on emotion and intelligence. Anyone can be clever, the trick is not to think the other guy is stupid.'

JOSÉ MOURINHO

'Coaching is not something I'm passionate about. I'm passionate about coaching kids.'

DAVID BECKHAM

'I'm going to tell you the story about the geese which fly 5,000 miles from Canada to France. They fly in V-formation but the second ones don't fly. They're the subs for the first ones. And then the second ones take over – so it's teamwork.'

ALEX FERGUSON

'If I fell into a barrel of boobs, I'd come out
sucking my thumb.'

IAN HOLLOWAY

'Sometimes you have to swallow the
unswallowable.'

ARSÈNE WENGER

'It's not important how we play. If you have
a Ferrari and I have a small car, to beat you
in a race I have to break your wheel or put
sugar in your tank.'

JOSÉ MOURINHO

'A football team is like a piano. You need
eight men to carry it and three who can
play the damn thing.'

BILL SHANKLY

THE STYLE COUNCIL

MONKS, FLOWERS AND PIANOS

'We don't want our players to be monks.
We want them to be better football players
because a monk doesn't play football at this
level.'

BOBBY ROBSON

'He dribbles a lot and the opposition don't
like it. You can see it all over their faces.'

RON ATKINSON

'It's all very well having a great pianist
playing, but it's no good if you haven't got
anyone to get the piano on the stage in the
first place – otherwise the pianist would be
standing there with no bloody piano to play.'

IAN HOLLOWAY

'Football is a more beautiful game in high
definition.'

JOSÉ MOURINHO

Interviewer: 'Would it be fair to describe you as a volatile player?'

Beckham: 'Well, I can play in the centre, on the right and occasionally on the left.'

'When you are surrounded by flowers, you breathe better.'

CRISTIANO RONALDO

'I have changed nothing, my style of play is still that of a child. I know that above all it is my job and that I should approach it in another way, but one must not lose sight of the fact that football is a game. It is imperative one plays to amuse oneself, to be happy. That is what children do and I do the same thing.'

LIONEL MESSI

'All this tippy-tappy stuff is all a load of b******s sometimes. Getting the ball into the opposition box as quickly as you can with quality is definitely sometimes the best way forward and that's what we did in the second half and that's why we won the game.'

SAM ALLARDYCE

'Zidane is unique. The ball flows with him. He is more like a dancer than a football player.'

ZINEDINE ZIDANE

'A great pianist doesn't run around the piano or do push-ups with his fingers. To be great, he plays the piano. Being a footballer is not about running, push-ups or physical work generally. The best way to be a great footballer is to play.'

JOSÉ MOURINHO

'Damien Delaney came in and did OK. I was hard on him, probably because I knew him and he was from Cork. I went over the top. I was the same with another lad, Colin Healy. He was from Cork, too, and I told him he was moving his feet like a League of Ireland player. It was wrong. Colin was new at the club. I should have been bending over backwards for him. I made the point about (Sunderland owner) Ellis Short talking to me like I was something on the bottom of his shoe. I think I spoke like that to some people at Ipswich.'

ROY KEANE

'There are only a few of us who can do that.'

PETER CROUCH REVIEWS A CRISTIANO RONALDO BICYCLE KICK

'I watched Arsenal in the Champions League the other week playing some of the best football I've ever seen and yet they couldn't have scored in a brothel with two grand in their pockets.'

IAN HOLLOWAY

'I'd waited long enough. I f*****g hit him hard. The ball was there (I think). Take that, you ****. And don't ever stand over me again sneering about fake injuries. And tell your pal (David) Wetherall there's some for him as well. I didn't wait for (ref) Mr Elleray to show the red card. I turned and walked to the dressing room. My attitude is an eye for an eye.'

ROY KEANE IN HIS AUTOBIOGRAPHY ON
ALF-INGE HAALAND

'The work of a team should always embrace a great player, but the great player must always work.'

ALEX FERGUSON

'They've picked their heads up off the ground – and they now have a lot to carry on their shoulders.'

RON ATKINSON

'In football you need to have everything in your cake mix to make the cake taste right. One little bit of ingredient that Tony (Pulis) uses in his cake that gets talked about all the time is Rory's (Delap) throw. Call that cinnamon and he's got a cinnamon-flavoured cake.'

IAN HOLLOWAY

John Terry was asked to describe what makes the ideal footballer. He said, 'A little bit of Joe Cole, and Zidane, with Beckham's right foot (for creativity). And Thierry Henry (for speed) but, 'Can I nominate (Claude) Makelele for his cock? It's huge! Like a beer can, it swings.'

IT'S REF JUSTICE

**DISCIPLINE, BALD BLOKES
AND WIVES**

'I was surprised we were playing in Manchester and to have a referee from Greater Manchester.'

BRENDAN RODGERS

'I don't understand referees. It appears like some players can't even be touched, but in my case, everyone can hit me as hard as they can.'

CRISTIANO RONALDO

'My wife runs the house much better than I could – so I think she could be a linesman or a referee or even a football manager and that's the truth.'

IAN HOLLOWAY

'You can't applaud a referee.'

ALEX FERGUSON

'This guy (Arsenal's Granit Xhaka) has become very disciplined although tonight he could get himself sent off.'

PAUL MERSON

'If Zizou kept his temper, he would not be the genius that he is.'

ZINEDINE ZIDANE

'I wouldn't want to get my pigeon chest out in front of anyone. I don't think the world needs it. I'd probably get a yellow card anyway.'

PETER CROUCH

'The trouble with referees is that they know the rules, but they do not know the game.'

BILL SHANKLY

'I shouldn't really say what I feel, but (ref Graham) Poll was their best midfielder in the goal. You saw him coming off at half-time and at the end. He smiled so much, he obviously enjoyed that performance. I think the referee should be banned.'

NEIL WARNOCK

'You are pushed to behave differently here (England), you don't really have a choice. If you cheat, you have no chance of being admired. Even your own supporters will dislike you. So what do you do? Well, the way is not to be stupid, but not to cheat either. If there is a foul, you have to fall. I call it helping the referee to make a decision. That's not cheating.'

JOSÉ MOURINHO

'I don't think there is any place in football for drinking. I have said on several occasions to players: You don't put diesel in a Ferrari.'

HARRY REDKNAPP

'They gave us four minutes (injury time) – that's an insult to the game. It denies you a proper chance to win a football match. There were six substitutions, the trainer came on, so that's four minutes right away and the goalkeeper must have wasted about two or three minutes and they took their time at every goal kick...the referee is responsible for time-keeping. It's ridiculous that it's 2012 and the referee still has control of that.'

ALEX FERGUSON

'When Tottenham striker Jimmy Greaves came out at Anfield, I handed him a piece of paper. He said: 'What's this?' I said: 'Just open it.' It was the menu from the Liverpool Infirmary.'

TOMMY SMITH

'David Elleray was that far away he would have needed binoculars. I really think it's about time we use the means to sort these things out rather than relying on some bald-headed bloke standing 50 yards away.'

NEIL WARNOCK

'It was lucky that the linesman wasn't stood in front of me as I would have poked him with a stick to make sure he was awake.'

IAN HOLLOWAY

'Unlike others who have been caught swearing on camera, I apologised immediately. And yet I am the only person banned for swearing. That doesn't seem right.'

WAYNE ROONEY

'Maybe Gary (Neville) deserves to be chased up a tunnel every now and then – there would be a queue for him, probably. But you have to draw a line eventually.'

ROY KEANE

'The pace of the game demanded a referee who was fit. It is an indictment of our game. You see referees abroad who are as fit as butcher's dogs. We have some who are fit. He (referee Alan Wiley) wasn't fit. He was taking thirty seconds to book a player. He was needing a rest. It was ridiculous.'

ALEX FERGUSON

INTERNATIONAL
RESCUE

**BULLS, HEADLIGHTS AND
A MOUSE**

'Someone in the England team will have to grab the ball by the horns.'

RON ATKINSON

'The World Cup is truly an international event.'

JOHN MOTSON

'Scotland have this habit of kicking themselves in the foot.'

ALAN BRAZIL

'I love playing for my country but my sanity is more important.'

ROY KEANE

THEY THINK IT'S ALL OVER

'Without being too harsh on Beckham, he cost us the match (against Argentina, World Cup 2002)'

IAN WRIGHT

'(Raymond) Domenech is the worst coach France have had since Louis XVI.'

ERIC CANTONA

'Samassi Abou don't speak the English too good.'

HARRY REDKNAPP

'She (Glenn Hoddle's faith healer) placed her hands on my shoulder and I said, 'Short back and sides, please, Eileen.'

RAY PARLOUR

'Germany are a very difficult team to play...
they had eleven internationals out there
today.'

STEVE LOMAS

'Now we have another two weeks to wait
to play our next game to let stupid football
associations make money from friendlies.'

SAM ALLARDYCE

Jimmy Hill: 'Don't sit on the fence, Terry,
what chance do you think Germany has of
getting through?'

Terry Venables: 'I think it's fifty-fifty.'

'I'm sure sex wouldn't be so rewarding as
this World Cup. It's not that sex isn't good,
but the World Cup is every four years and
sex is not.'

BRAZILIAN RONALDO

'I've signed a contract with the Dutch national team until 2006, so I can win the World Cup not once but twice.'

LOUIS VAN GAAL

'I'm ready to lose my life if that's what Portugal needs to win. I'll play against the USA even if I play with one leg.'

CRISTIANO RONALDO

'We (Scotland) absolutely annihilated England. It was a massacre. We beat them 5–4.'

BILL SHANKLY

'In France, everybody realised that God exists, and that he is back in the French international team. God is back, there is little left to say.'

ZIDANE ON ZIDANE

'I think the most important goal I scored in Spain was the first one because people were wary about me coming over to Spain as a player. They thought I was just there to sell shirts.'

DAVID BECKHAM

'I don't speak foreign languages. I find f*** off is understood by pretty much anyone.'

BRIAN CLOUGH

'I wasn't as fit as I would have liked to have been, going to the World Cup, but I'm not sure what difference that made.'

DAVID BECKHAM

'I didn't see the England game live, but I did see the headlights.'

ALAN BRAZIL

'Superstitions aren't designed to make
sense. Before England games, John Terry
would refuse to touch a ball with his feet in
the dressing room. Every time a ball came
near him he'd freak out. A rolling ball would
see him lift both feet off the floor, like an old
dear with a mouse.'

PETER CROUCH

'Who do you (Mick McCarthy) think you
are having meetings about me? You were a
cr*p player and you are a cr*p manager. The
only reason I have any dealings with you is
that somehow you are the manager of my
country and you're not even Irish,
you English ****!'

ROY KEANE

INJURIES AND BUILD

PELÉ, HAIRCUTS AND RATS

'I don't have any tattoos, but that's mainly because none of my limbs are wide enough to support a visible image.'

PETER CROUCH

'That's great, tell him he's Pelé and get him back on.'

PARTICK THISTLE BOSS JOHN LAMBIE IS TOLD HIS PLAYER WAS CONCUSSED AND HAD FORGOTTEN WHO HE WAS

'I have come to accept that if I have a new haircut it is front page news. But having a picture of my foot on the front page of a national newspaper is a bit exceptional.'

DAVID BECKHAM ON ENGLAND FANS PRAYING HE WOULD BE FIT FOR THE WORLD CUP

'Sandro's holding his face, from that you can tell it's a knee injury.'

DION DUBLIN

'For many years I have thought he (El Hadji Diouf) was the gutter type – I was going to call him a sewer rat, but that might be insulting to sewer rats. He's the lowest of the low and I can't see him being at Blackburn much longer.'

NEIL WARNOCK AFTER THE STRIKER MOCKED AN INJURED RIVAL

'(Shaun) Derry would insist on being sick before every game. By which I mean, if the nerves hadn't naturally made him sick, he would stick his fingers down his throat and do the job himself. At the risk of stating the obvious, it really killed the Portsmouth dressing-room vibe.'

PETER CROUCH

'I took a whack on my left ankle, but something told me it was my right.'

LEE HENDRIE

'(Stephen) Hunt has proved on a few occasions that he's a clever type, and his challenge on Nick Montgomery earlier in the game wasn't clever either.'

NEIL WARNOCK

'No, Wayne (Rooney) doesn't need it (tips about style). He has his own style. But with hair he looks much better. He looks very good now. Before, he was a little bit ugly, but now, with hair, he's beautiful.'

IAN HOLLOWAY

'On a night we got beaten in the cup by Luton, the staff came in and said, 'Clive Clarke has had a heart attack at Leicester.' I said, 'Is he OK? I'm shocked they found one, you could never tell by the way he plays.''

ROY KEANE

David Beckham was so keen to get his first son Brooklyn into football he had him wearing a Man United football kit in bed. He also made sure his son watched him in garden kickabouts, before he could walk. One day, just after he'd started standing unhindered, David found him in the kitchen kicking at a ball as he'd seen dad do. It was only when he fell on the floor crying that Becks realised his eager-to-please lad had, in fact, kicked a can of baked beans.

Big Sam Allardyce says that Ian Greaves, his first manager at Bolton in the 1970s, promised him £50 if he burst the ball in a tackle. But despite his efforts to go in extra hard on opposing strikers, to his regret, he never managed to claim the cash.

THE STAR MEN

FENCES, ROCKS AND LEG-BREAKERS

'I believe a young player will run through a barbed-wire fence for you. An older player looks for a hole in the fence, he'll try and get his way through it some way, but the young player will fight for you.'

BRENDAN RODGERS

'Tony Adams is the rock that the team has grown from.'

RON ATKINSON

'I wouldn't touch Chimbonda with a barn door.'

ALAN BRAZIL

'I think Charlie George was one of Arsenal's all-time great players. A lot of people might not agree with that, but I personally do.'

JIMMY GREAVES

'It took a lot of bottle for Tony to own
up to it.'

IAN WRIGHT ON TONY ADAMS'
ALCOHOLISM

'You can say that strikers are very much like
postmen – they have to get in and out as
quick as they can before the dog starts to
have a go.'

IAN HOLLOWAY

'(Danny) Welbeck is not the standard
required at Manchester United.'

LOUIS VAN GAAL

'Kevin Muscat scared me. You know, people
would say, 'I'm going to break your legs'.
When he would say it, you genuinely
believed him.'

PETER CROUCH

'There have been a few players described as the new George Best over the years, but this is the first time it's been a compliment to me.'

GEORGE BEST ON CRISTIANO RONALDO

'Whether dribbling or sprinting, Ryan (Giggs) can leave the best defenders with twisted blood.'

ALEX FERGUSON

'We grow our players at this club. We don't have a greenhouse in the back because we can't afford it – we're more of a microwave club.'

WATFORD MANAGER AIDY BOOTHROYD

'I don't think I look up to any players. Obviously you respect everyone.'

WAYNE ROONEY

'I feel close to the rebelliousness of the youth here. Perhaps time will separate us, but nobody can deny that here, behind the windows of Manchester, there is an insane love of football, of celebration and of music.'

ERIC CANTONA

'(Brazilian) Ronaldo was my hero. I loved watching players like Zidane, Ronaldinho and Rivaldo, but Ronaldo was the best striker I've ever seen. He was so fast, he could score from nothing and could shoot the ball better than anyone I've ever seen.'

LIONEL MESSI

'Iniesta doesn't dye his hair, he doesn't wear earrings and he hasn't got any tattoos. Maybe that makes him unattractive to the media, but he is the best.'

PEP GUARDIOLA

'Fergie said I was a Man United player in the wrong shirt. I said he was an Arsenal manager in the wrong blazer.'

TONY ADAMS

'I'm a prince and I'm sort of slaying a dragon, which is something I've never done before, obviously.'

DAVID BECKHAM ON HIS APPEARANCE IN A DISNEY ADVERT

'I remember the first time I saw him (Giggs). He was thirteen and just floated over the ground like a cocker spaniel chasing a piece of silver paper in the wind.'

ALEX FERGUSON

'I don't even know who Joey Barton is.'

NEYMAR

'Tom Finney would have been great in any team, in any match and in any age, even if he had been wearing an overcoat.'

BILL SHANKLY

'I've told him (David Seaman) to cut off his ponytail. I think it makes him less aerodynamic.'

ARSÈNE WENGER

'Zidane is one of the greatest players in history, a truly magnificent player.'

ZIDANE ON ZIDANE

'He (Dennis Wise) could start a row in an empty house.'

ALEX FERGUSON

'(Philipp) Lahm is a scandal. He is super-intelligent, understands the game brilliantly, knows when to come inside or to stay wide. The guy is f*****g exceptional.'

PEP GUARDIOLA

'The tackle from Matthew Upson was on a par with the referee.'

READING'S DAVE KITSON

'I've only been to Wembley once. It was about five years ago – Lenny Kravitz at Wembley Arena.'

FULHAM BOSS CHRIS COLEMAN

'I like to watch good football so I like to watch good players. I like Cristiano Ronaldo, Andrés Iniesta, Xavi and Wayne Rooney.'

NEYMAR

'Paddy (Kenny) has a balloon on his forehead like you have never seen. If somebody headbutted me like somebody has headbutted Kenny, then I would chin him.'

NEIL WARNOCK

'Wayne's like my son, Brooklyn, who goes out in the garden to play and have fun.'

DAVID BECKHAM

'Rooney's touch is so good it's like he's got velvet gloves on his feet.'

IAIN DOWIE

'If he (Gary Neville) was an inch taller, he'd be the best centre-half in Britain. His father is 6ft 2in – I'd check the milkman.'

ALEX FERGUSON

'He (Harry Kane) is part of the problem, he's on the pitch, he needs to do more.'

ROY KEANE ON WHETHER SPURS' POOR RESULTS WOULD MAKE KANE LEAVE

'I'd go as far as to say they (Chelsea) got themselves the division's second best-looking target man.'

PETER CROUCH ON OLIVIER GIROUD

'He's going to be what? Oh, for god's sake. Sir David Beckham? You're having a laugh. He's just a good footballer with a famous bird.'

IAN HOLLOWAY

Brazil's Ronaldo swapped shirts with David Beckham after a match against England. The Brazilian later revealed he was shocked by the state of the shirt, saying, 'Normally they are soaked in sweat and stink, but Beckham's shirt smelled of perfume.'

Pablo Zabaleta was rollocked by Lionel Messi after he drove his fellow Argentine home after Messi fell asleep in his car after a meal out in Barcelona. He told the *Daily Mail*, 'I asked him: "Leo, before you sleep, where do I take you?" "To my house in Castel de Fels," he said, and he fell asleep. We arrived at his house and I woke Leo up and he said: "Not here! I told you my other house!"'

THE FOREIGN LEGION

PASTA, HOTEL FIRES AND A HITMAN

'That shot is impossible. I saw Yaya Touré do it once.'

MICHAEL OWEN

'He (Júlio Baptista) has that smell to be where he needs to be at the decisive moment. When there is chocolate to take in the box he is there.'

ARSÈNE WENGER

'He was a quiet man, Eric Cantona, but he was a man of few words.'

DAVID BECKHAM

'When an Italian says it's pasta, I check under the sauce to make sure. They are innovators of the smokescreen.'

ALEX FERGUSON

Southampton boss Lawrie McMenemy started to draw a ball and a goal on a blackboard and spoke slowly at newcomer Ivan Golac's first team tactics meeting. Captain Alan Ball said: 'Don't be silly, boss – Ivan speaks perfect English.' McMenemy replied: 'I'm not doing this for him. I'm doing it for the rest of you!'

'I like (Mario) Balotelli – he's even crazier than me. He can score a winner, then set fire to the hotel.'

ZLATAN IBRAHIMOVIĆ

'I wouldn't say that he (David Ginola) is the best winger in the Premiership, but there are none better.'

RON ATKINSON

'It was like living in a foreign country.'

***IAN RUSH ON HIS LIFE AT JUVENTUS
IN ITALY***

'(Olivier) Giroud scored an unbelievable header with the last kick of the game.'

CHRIS KAMARA

'Why do you want Zidane, when we have Tim Sherwood?'

BLACKBURN OWNER JACK WALKER

'Sandro's holding his face. You can tell from that it's a knee injury.'

DION DUBLIN

'That lad (Filippo Inzaghi) must have been born offside.'

ALEX FERGUSON

'It's my country but I don't want to know about France. I was born there but I feel English.'

ERIC CANTONA

'I tape over most of them with *Corrie* or *Neighbours*. Most of them are crap. They can f*****g make anyone look good. I signed Marco Boogers off a video. He was a good player but a nutter. They didn't show that on the video.'

HARRY REDKNAPP

'I wasn't good enough. That is the truth. I was old, really old as a football player. I knocked on the door (at Wigan), I tried to come here to play in English football as a player, but I was not able. The same happened here at Man City. They were so clever!'

PEP GUARDIOLA

'The problem with Chelsea is I lack a striker. I have Samuel Eto'o but he is 32 years old, maybe 35, who knows?'

JOSÉ MOURINHO

'If it had come to a fight, Patrick (Vieira) could probably have killed me.'

ROY KEANE

'Pelé was a complete player. I didn't see him live obviously, because I wasn't born.'

DAVID BECKHAM

'Cristiano (Ronaldo) reminds me of German tennis player Michael Stich. He was destined to make history, but then Boris Becker showed up. Cristiano is so fast, so strong, so incredible, but he has one problem: Leo Messi.'

JÜRGEN KLOPP

'I think he (Benitez) was an angry man. He must have been disturbed for some reason. I think you have got to cut through the venom of it and hopefully he'll reflect and understand what he said was absolutely ridiculous.'

ALEX FERGUSON

'People that really know me, they adore me.'

CRISTIANO RONALDO, BLEACHERREPORT.COM

'He's a novice, he (Wenger) should keep his opinions to Japanese football.'

ALEX FERGUSON

'You can't find Tony Adams. He's disappeared to Azerbaijan, or somewhere ridiculous in the world.'

HARRY REDKNAPP

'Will I become a coach in the future?
No way, I'd never be able to put up with
someone like me.'

ROMÁRIO

'He (Peter Schmeichel) was towering over
me and the other players were almost
covering their eyes. I'm looking up and
thinking, 'If he does hit me, I'm dead.'

ALEX FERGUSON

When Robin van Persie first started dating
future wife Bouchra, he shocked her by
admitting he slept with a couple of footballs
in his bed.

Russian linesman Tofiq Bakhramov told ref Gottfried Dienst that Geoff Hurst's crossbar goal in the 1966 World Cup final should stand, making it 3–2 as England went on to win their only World Cup. He had ignored strong protests from West Germany's players and when asked some time later why he had done so, replied, 'Stalingrad' – a reference to World War Two.

Late Arsenal star José Antonio Reyes used to practise dribbling in his North London home's garden with large plastic gnomes dotted around – in an attempt to fit in with what he viewed as how an English footballer lived.

Mario Balotelli left behind one final reminder of his maverick nature when he departed Man City in 2013. Former club kitman Les Chapman said, 'He used to wonder why his car was impounded twenty-seven times – because it was painted in camouflage and he parked it on double yellows outside San Carlo restaurant in the middle of Manchester every day. (Then) I opened his locker after he left and all his parking tickets just fell out!'

ABOUT THE AUTHOR

Frank Worrall is a British journalist and author. He was born in Bury, north Manchester, and moved to London to work for national newspapers. He has written regularly for *The Sun*, *The Sunday Times* and the *Mail on Sunday*. Frank is also the author of eighteen books on sport, including the bestselling *Lewis Hamilton: The Definitive Biography*, *Roy Keane: Red Man Walking*, *Rooney*, *Celtic United*, *Jamie Vardy*, and *Rory McIlroy*. In the 1980s, he was renowned for his work in music journalism, producing the first ever interviews with New Order, Pulp and Morrissey. In 2012, Frank published his first novel, *Elvis Has Left The Building*. This is his first foray into compiling a book designed with the sole ambition of making you chuckle – we hope it did just that. His website is Frankworrall.com

And here, Frank signs off with a brief Q&A of his personal loves and pet hates of the beautiful game, which goes like this...

Q. Who do you support and why?

A. I'm embarrassed to admit this but I started out supporting Man City from a distance as a boy, because I liked the sky blue colour of their shirt! I moved on to Bury FC, my local team, when I was old enough to attend matches and then joined the big boys, transferring my colours to Man United. Yes, I know.

Q. What was your worst moment in football?

A. Crying on the steps of the old Wembley in 1976 after Bobby Stokes smashed Man United's dream of winning the FA Cup.

Q. And your best?

A. Seeing George Best at Old Trafford when I was very young, perched on my dad's shoulders. The memory image is black and white, but George's sheer artistry turns it to colour.

Q. Who are the best footballers you have seen live?

A. 1. Diego Maradona. 2. George Best. 3. Cristiano Ronaldo. 4. Lionel Messi. 5. Ronaldihno. 6. Colin Bell. 7. Kenny Dalglish. 8. Bryan Robson. 9. Eric Cantona. 10. Derek Spence (leftfield choice, I know, but a Bury great).

Q. What is the most puzzling thing in the modern game?

A. Why Man City and PSG still can't win the Champions League given the quality of their squads and riches. Additionally, why Pep Guardiola can't win it without Messi – I know it riles him when people say that.

Q. Which modern era player could easily perform just as effectively in the pre-Prem days, and vice-versa.

A. I think you could swap Kevin de Bruyne and Colin Bell. Both midfield maestros and with the same energy that earned Colin the nickname, Nijinksy (after the famous racehorse).

179

THEY THINK IT'S ALL OVER

Q. Who is the greatest English top-flight manager ever?

A. Total trophy hauls would suggest Alex Ferguson and Bob Paisley, but for me it is Brian Clough. To win the European Cup (the pre-glam version of the Champions League) with Nottingham Forest is arguably the top achievement of any manager.

Q. What do we need more and less of in today's football?

A. More respect, and less abuse, of referees. More hi-tech stadia like Tottenham's and less like Man United's creaking Old Trafford. Cheaper tickets for fans and for TV satellite viewing. More respect from blokes for the women's game, especially after England women's Euro 2022 exploits. And less bad language on the terraces... how would you feel if it was your ten-year-old taking it all in?

Q. Finally...what's a particular pet hate of yours about football?

A. This may sound snobby, but poor language skills from pundits. Phrases such as the cliché 'at the end of the day', 'we'll go for *them* three points' (copyright Glenn Hoddle), '*Listen*' to stress emphasis at the start a sentence (copyright Trevor Sinclair), '*I was like, he/ she was like*' as a preface to an anecdote, and the killer, '*I'm not gonna lie*' (copyright Love Island and Rebecca Vardy). Come on guys – and girls – you can do better, and we deserve better. Rant over. *Thank you, and goodnight.*